Can You Hear Us?

A collection of poems centred on listening to the voices of children, their thoughts and reflections.

Mabellyn Dennis

Crafted
INSPIRATION

Can You Hear Us?
A collection of poems centred on listening to the voices of children, their thoughts and reflections.

First published in Great Britain in 2020 by Crafted Inspiration

Crafted Inspiration
Email: maybelline@craftedinspiration.co.uk

ISBN: 978-1-64999-161-4

CONTENTS

Introduction

Can You Hear Us, is a collection of poems which gives voice to children's thoughts, views and reflections. For many years practitioners working with children have communicated their challenges when attempting to understand the most appropriate ways in which to engage and listen to children's voices and give them a platform to be heard.

Concerns and interest for this area of development has found expression in practitioners exploring different methods and attending forums to seek answers to understand how to listen to children's voices.

Listening to the voice of the child has been a dominant focus of policy for many years and its importance is rooted in the United Nations Convention on the Rights of the Child (UNCRC, 1989) 'Article 12', which places emphasis on the importance of children having the right to their voices being heard.

It is hoped that this collection of poems will provide everyone working with children and young people a creative way to listen to their voices, safeguard them, build self-esteem and at the same time gain a greater awareness of their needs.

Acknowledgements

I would like to thank everyone who has supported me through their prayers, encouragement, time and resources for the completion of this book. Most of all I want to thank God for the gift of inspiration and creativity.

To my Pastors Matthew and Yemisi Ashimolowo, your wisdom, support, encouragement and confidence in my creative abilities has provided me with the opportunity to shine. I am truly grateful. Thank you, Pastor Ade D'Almeida for your support and being a constant source of knowledge, inspiration and encouragement.

To my siblings Delroy, David and Trisha, thank you for teaching me the importance of listening to children.

To my dear friends, Grace Fagan, Donna Thomas, Christie John-Baptiste, Cathrina Oshinowo and Mary Robinson, thank you for the amazing opportunities which you have provided for me to create poetry and engage in unique projects in the UK and the Caribbean to listen to the voices of children.

Tracey Linton, Joan Sutherland -Tweed, Mavis Madzingira, Lombe Sichangwa, Tobi and Arinola Alabi, I am so grateful for your input of encouragement and resources. Thank you Tanisha Darling for your skills in photography and providing the photograph for the cover of the book.

Uncle George, Noel and our departed Errol you have been inspirational. To my wonderful aunties, Ellen, Clara, Elvira and Edith, you have always taken the time to listen to me, thank you. Joseph Ademosu I am grateful for your encouragement, support and patience, whilst working with me on this project.

To my mother, beautiful Mary thank you for allowing my poems to take a place of pride in your home.

Above all I want to especially thank my husband Karl for being my greatest encourager and supporter. You identified my ability to encourage and inspire others and have taken the time to listen, review, organise and helped to shape every poem which I have written, I am truly thankful.

Endorsements

The poems strike me as items that can be used as a workbook for Young People and Practitioners with optional tasks as a group or individually. When reading each one it offers an opportunity for discussion but also self-reflection. This could also be used as a tool for practitioners to look behind the messages in the statement.

Grace Fagan

Safeguarding Consultant for Children and Families

A perceptive collection of writings that offers insight into particular discourses, self-identity; self-esteem and belonging. The poems titled *'I love the look of me'*, *'Faces'* and *'You may not know'* will resonate with anyone who has ever felt marginalised, offering instead recognition, acceptance and liberty.

Donna Thomas

Head of Early Years and Early Help

Dedication

I would like to dedicate this book to my children Marcus, Serene, Yewah, and Jawanza. To Asher, my grandson and all the children and young people with whom I have had the pleasure of working with and who have provided me with the opportunity to engage in listening to their voices.

You Don't Listen

You don't listen when I speak to you
What more can I really do?
You don't listen to the tears I cry
or when I take my deepest sigh
My thoughts, my life are in your hands.

Why don't you hear when I cry out?
Is there nothing for me to shout about?
Just stop one minute and hear my heart
Please don't wait until we part
You don't listen when I speak to you
What more can I really do?

Reflections:

Listening to children builds their confidence.

Speak To Me

Speak very slowly
Help me to understand
Take a look into my eyes
Signal with your hand
Show a little patience
Use a little calm
Show a little care
Help remove my every fear.

Reflections:

There are many ways to communicate and listen.

I Tried To Speak To You

I tried to speak to you today
You rushed around I felt a way.
I tried to tell you how I feel
About the world and my deepest needs.
I spoke in whispers small and still
I spoke as cymbals clanging loud.
Yet all my words could not be heard.

Oh, hush you said I am busy now
In just one minute I will hear you out.
Your minute lasted for one year
The day was here but the night drew near.
I tried to speak to you today
Yet again you had no time for me I say.

Reflections:

Encourage children and young people to share their experiences, views and reflections.

Children

There are children all around us
Listen and you will hear
The sounds that they are making
Echoing in your ear.
The children all around us
Need love and tender care
Don't silence the sounds they are making
And fill their lives with fear.

Reflections:

Listen to the stories of children.

Footsteps Of A Child

Walk in the footsteps of a child
That is what we need to do
Walk in the footsteps of a child
Hold their hand and see them through
Walk in the footsteps of a child
Give confidence, joy and hope
Walk in the footsteps of a child
Relieve their pain
Restore their smile.

Reflections:

Undivided attention is the key to successful communication.

Communication

Silence communicates
Talking communicates
Whispers communicate
Shouting communicates.

Anger communicates
Tears communicate
Fear communicates
Pain communicates.

Smiles communicate
Laughter communicates
Praise communicates
How do you communicate?

Reflections:

Positive communication can help develop a positive self-esteem.

Children's Voices

Listen very carefully to the voices all around
Those who communicate in silence
As they cannot make a sound
We need to hear their messages that do not
come with words
Listen very carefully to the voices
All around.

Reflections:

Every child is an individual.

Listen

Our children often speak to us
In more words than we can tell
If only we would take the time
To listen very well.
Children simply want to tell
Of experiences in their day
Stop. Look. Listen.
To what they have to say.

Reflections:

Listen with your eyes, ears and emotions.

We Matter

I matter you matter
Come on and tell the world
I matter you matter
Every boy and every girl
I matter you matter
Shout it loud and clear
I matter you matter
Let everybody hear.

Reflections:

Listen to the voices of children.

You May Not Know

You may not know just how it feels
to be waiting on the restless seas.
In a boat so old and worn
drifting away from those we mourn.

You may feel the need to criticise
Pass judgment and want to minimise.
The experiences faced by those in boats
Trying desperately to survive and stay
afloat.

Don't judge for you cannot see
The pain and pressure inside of me.
You cannot imagine just how it feels
When all you have is lost at sea.

Reflections:

Be kind and considerate not judgemental.

Play

Give me a chance to play
Monday, Tuesday, every day.
Give me a chance to say
About the kinds of play
I need to have today.

Play is great and play is fun
Play gives me the chance to run, run, run.
Gives me a chance to play
Wednesday, Thursday, Friday,
Saturday, Sunday, every day, any day.

I want to play, explore the world and
roam
I want to play until I am grown
I want to play and have great fun
I want to play don't stop me now.

Reflections:

Play strengthens our emotional and physical muscles. It also stimulates the imagination.

I Like The Look Of Me

I look into the mirror; beauty is what I see.
Skin so perfectly coloured, I like the look of me.
Eyes that shine so brightly, teeth all glistening white,
I am the image of excellence; I love the look of me.

Reflections:

Encourage confidence through praise.

Faces

I see so many faces in this world around
I see so many faces wanting to be found.

I see so many faces glaring back at me
I see so many faces waiting to be free.

Faces with smiles don't mind waiting a while
Faces with frowns always putting you down.

Faces with endurance, despite the challenges of life
Faces filled with tears, desperation and grief.

Faces are the voices hidden from the world
Listen to them carefully and their stories will unfold.

Reflections:

There are many positive ways to communicate and listen, find one.

I am Speaking

I am speaking so that you can hear
I am speaking loudly in your ear.
I am speaking things you have never heard
Of stories, and experiences that are blurred.

I am speaking things you need to know
I am speaking stuff from long ago.
I am speaking because I want to speak
I am speaking because I need to speak.

Reflections:

Children are good communicators let them speak.

Praise

You praise the children, every one
It doesn't matter if they are slow or fast.
You praise them when they come in first
And even when they come in last.

You praise them in the morning sun
You praise them when their day is done.
You praise them when they are still small.
You praise them when they grow up tall.

Reflections:

Celebrate a child's achievement no matter how small.

I Can Achieve

You said I could, you said I would
Achieve the best in life.
You said I could, you said I would
Fulfil my dreams inside.
You looked at me and you saw
All the things I want to be
And told me that I will achieve
The things I see inside of me.

Reflections:

Positive affirmation and encouragement help to build confidence

You Make A Difference

You have made a difference
In what you do and say.
You have made a difference
In children's lives each day.
You have made a difference
To every family.
You have made a difference
With your positive energy.

Reflections:

Help to make a difference in the life of a child.

Speak

Speak a word of kindness
Speak your words with care
Speak words of praise
Remove doubt and fear
Speak a word of courage
Speak a word that builds
Speak a word of thankfulness
And create my atmosphere.

Reflections:

Use positive words when speaking

Our Voices

Our voices cannot be silenced
Our message is loud and clear
Against hunger and injustice
War, hatred and fear.

Our voices are the channel
From which changes can flow
Let our voices echo, everywhere we go.
Echo, echo, echo everywhere we go.

Reflections:

Children and young people have rights,
help to protect them.

CPSIA information can be obtained
at www.ICGtesting.com
Printed in the USA
LVHW092001091220
673739LV00004B/14

9 781649 991614